GALACTIC
Geometry

Lisa Arias

Rourke
Educational Media

rourkeeducationalmedia.com

Scan for Related Titles
and Teacher Resources

Before Reading:

Building Academic Vocabulary and Background Knowledge

Before reading a book, it is important to tap into what your child or students already know about the topic. This will help them develop their vocabulary, increase their reading comprehension, and make connections across the curriculum.

1. *Look at the cover of the book. What will this book be about?*
2. *What do you already know about the topic?*
3. *Let's study the Table of Contents. What will you learn about in the book's chapters?*
4. *What would you like to learn about this topic? Do you think you might learn about it from this book? Why or why not?*
5. *Use a reading journal to write about your knowledge of this topic. Record what you already know about the topic and what you hope to learn about the topic.*
6. *Read the book.*
7. *In your reading journal, record what you learned about the topic and your response to the book.*
8. *After reading the book complete the activities below.*

Content Area Vocabulary
Read the list. What do these words mean?

area
dimensions
distributive property
height
length
parallel
parallelograms
perimeter
points
polygon
quadrilateral
3-dimensional
2-dimensional
width

After Reading:

Comprehension and Extension Activity

After reading the book, work on the following questions with your child or students in order to check their level of reading comprehension and content mastery.

1. *Why is a triangle a polygon but not a heart? (Asking questions)*
2. *Explain the difference between area and perimeter. (Summarize)*
3. *Why are symbols used in geometry? (Asking questions)*
4. *What is the difference between 2-dimensional and 3-dimensional? (Summarize)*
5. *What are some items in your home or school that are quadrilaterals? (Text to self connection)*

Extension Activity

Find the perimeter of a room in your house or a space in your classroom. Before you start, make an educated guess on what the perimeter will be and write it down. Then gather your materials. You will need a tape measure, pencil, and paper. Do you remember how you find the perimeter? Measure all sides of a shape, such as your square bedroom, and add them together. What is the perimeter of your room? Is the perimeter close to your guess?

TABLE OF CONTENTS.

DIMENSIONS

Get ready to discover and uncover the **properties** of shapes.

Take a moment to compare the shapes seen here.

Before we begin, let's get warmed up and learn about **dimensions**.

Points allow you to see
the exact location of where they should be.
A point has no measure or dimension,
just simply its position.

length

Lines are one-dimensional and
have just one measure... **length**.

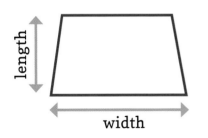

Plane shapes are so clever.
They bring length and **width** together.
Because of this fact,
2-dimensional shapes are always flat.

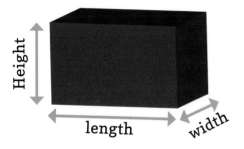

Solid shapes are even better.
They join three measures together.
Height, length, and width are the
measures that create **3-dimensional**
shapes with pleasure.

POLYGONS

Let's take a moment to see
what polygons mean to you and me.

Polygons are closed 2-dimensional shapes with straight sides.

Check It Out!

Open   Closed

Is it a **polygon** or not?
Explain why a shape is not a polygon.

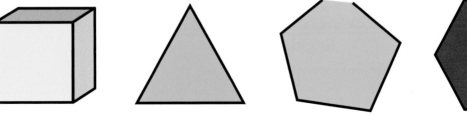

Polygons are just like a game.
The number of sides gives them their name.

Regular polygons have all equal sides and irregular polygons do not.

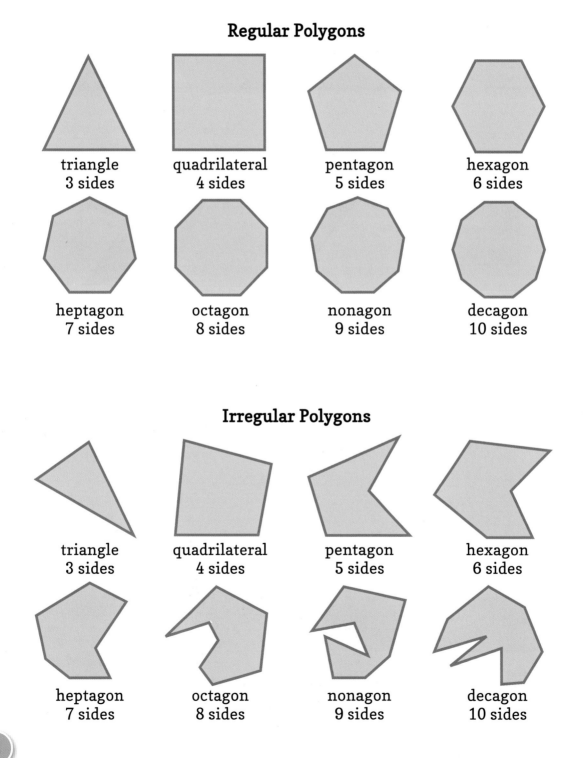

Regular Polygons

triangle
3 sides

quadrilateral
4 sides

pentagon
5 sides

hexagon
6 sides

heptagon
7 sides

octagon
8 sides

nonagon
9 sides

decagon
10 sides

Irregular Polygons

triangle
3 sides

quadrilateral
4 sides

pentagon
5 sides

hexagon
6 sides

heptagon
7 sides

octagon
8 sides

nonagon
9 sides

decagon
10 sides

8

6

Answers:

Regular pentagon: 5 equal sides.	Irregular quadrilateral: unequal sides.
Regular triangle: 3 equal sides.	
Irregular hexagon: 6 unequal sides.	Irregular quadrilateral: 4 unequal sides.
Irregular pentagon: 5 unequal sides.	
Regular quadrilateral: 4 equal sides.	Irregular pentagon: 5 unequal sides.
Irregular triangle: 3 unequal sides.	

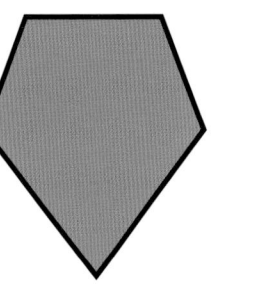  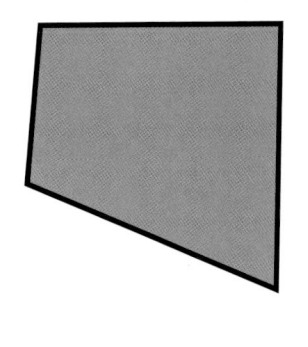

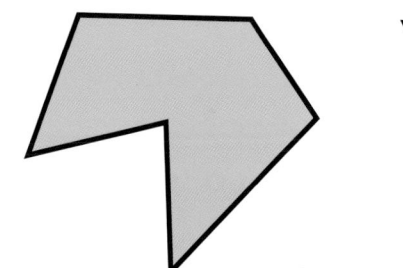 

Name each polygon, decide if it is regular or irregular, and explain why.

Quadrilaterals

A **quadrilateral** is any polygon with four sides.
Quadrilaterals include all types of kites, trapezoids,
parallelograms, and any other four-sided shape that you create.

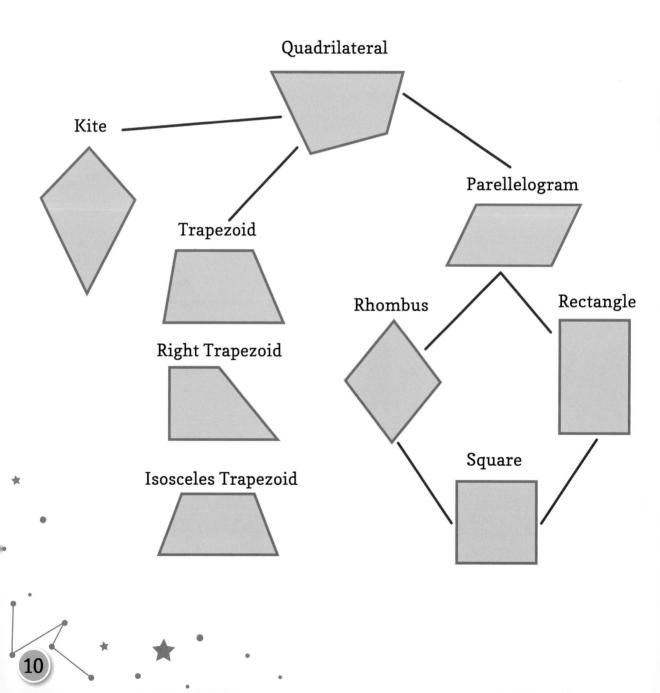

Comparing quadrilaterals by sides and angles is easy to do
when the shapes are marked with special symbols for me and you.

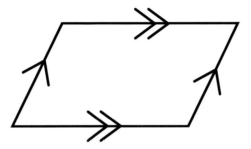

Matching arrows show that sides are **parallel**. Parallel lines run in
the same direction, but never touch.

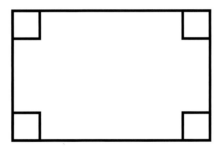

Corners that are 90 degrees are marked with a box.

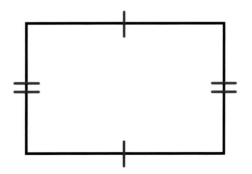

Sides with lines, show they are equal.

Parallelograms

Parallelograms are quadrilaterals with two pairs
of parallel sides.

Many parallelograms are found in the quadrilateral set.

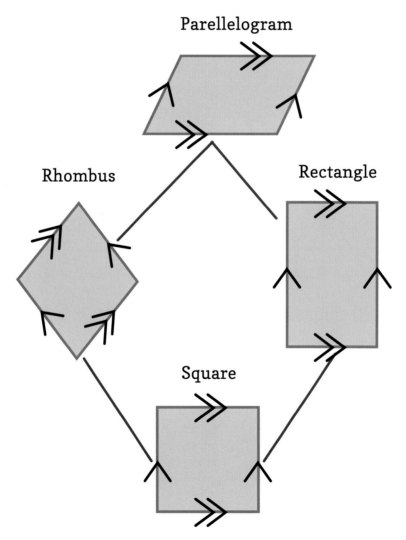

Rectangles, rhombuses, and squares are all parallelograms.

Angles are important factors to see
when comparing shapes for you and me.

Let's give it a try and organize parallelograms
by angle and side.

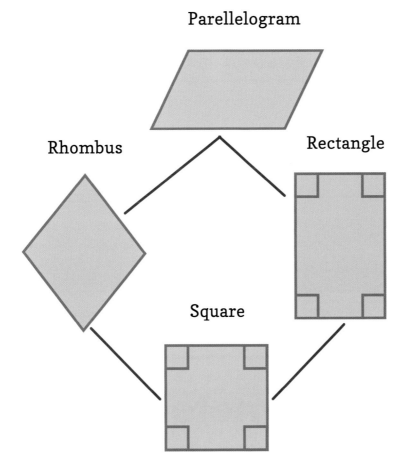

Parellelogram

Rhombus

Rectangle

Square

In the parallelogram family, rectangles and
squares have four right angles.

Squares have a bit more flare
with four equal sides to compare.

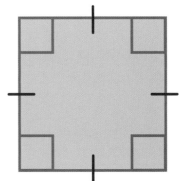

PERIMETER OF SHAPES

The **perimeter** is the distance around the outside of a shape.

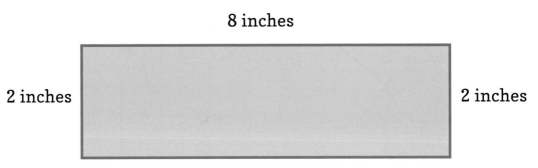

8 inches

2 inches   2 inches

8 inches

Perimeter:

$$8 + 2 + 8 + 2 = 20$$

To find the perimeter of a shape, add the measures of every side together.

Find the perimeter of each shape.

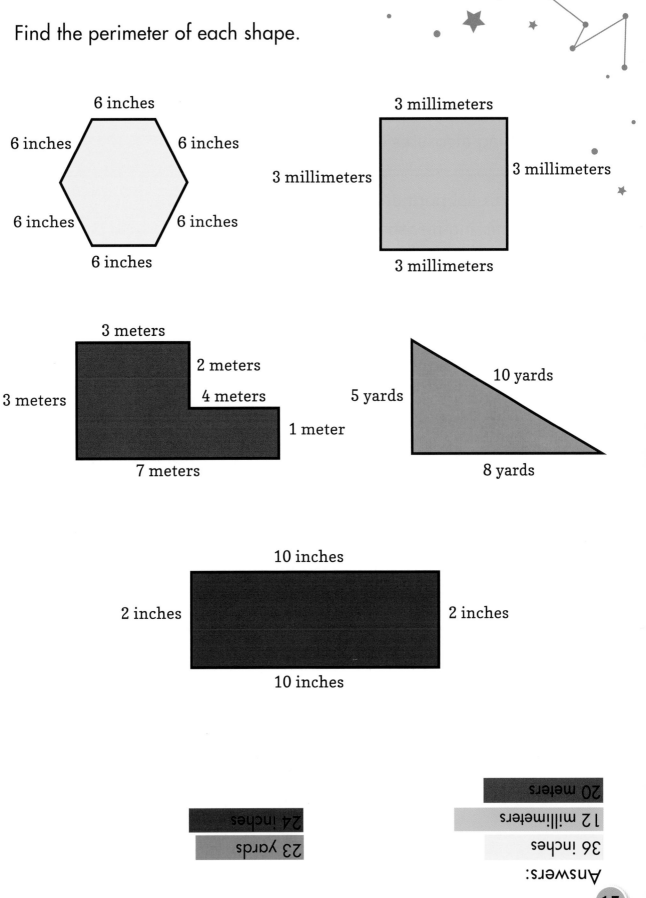

6 inches
6 inches   6 inches
6 inches   6 inches
6 inches

3 millimeters
3 millimeters   3 millimeters
3 millimeters

3 meters
2 meters
4 meters
3 meters
1 meter
7 meters

10 yards
5 yards
8 yards

10 inches
2 inches   2 inches
10 inches

Missing Measures

Finding the perimeter can be done
even if missing measures are on the run!

Matching parallel partners is what you do
to find the missing measures for me and you.

For any missing side, look across the shape to find its mate.

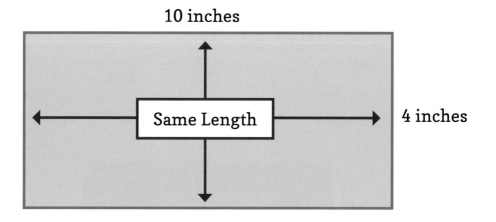

Perimeter:

10 + 10 + 4 + 4 = 28 inches

Find the perimeter of each shape.

12 centimeters

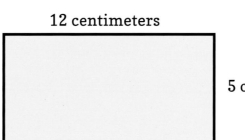

5 centimeters

8 meters

5 meters

8 meters

5 inches

Here is what to do to find missing measures when the perimeter is given to you. To find the missing sides, use the properties of shapes and parallel sides and work in reverse.

Perimeter = 20 centimeters

Squares have equal sides. 20 ÷ 4 = 5, so each side is equal to 5 centimeters.

The opposite sides of rectangles are equal, so all that needs to be done is to subtract the sides that are known and split what is left in half.

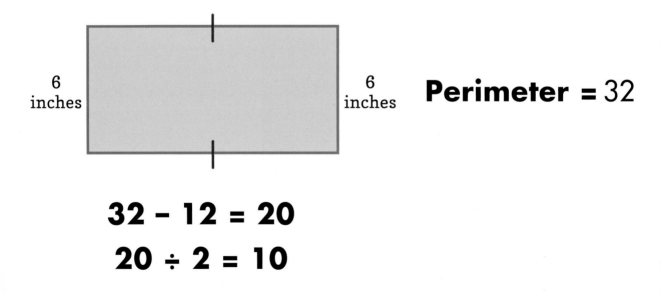

6 inches   6 inches   **Perimeter =** 32

32 – 12 = 20

20 ÷ 2 = 10

The remaining sides of the rectangle are 10 inches.

Find the missing side measures.

Perimeter = 16 centimeters

Perimeter = 22 inches

9 inches

Perimeter = 36 yards

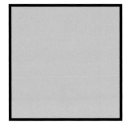

Perimeter = 16 feet

6 feet

AREA OF SHAPES

Area is a measure that shows just what it takes to cover up shapes.

To find the area, count the number of square units inside a shape.

1	2	3	4	5
6	7	8	9	10
11	12	13	14	15
16	17	18	19	20

1	2
3	4
5	6
7	8
9	10
11	12

1	2	3	4
5	6	7	8

In a hurry?
No need to worry.
Multiplying is the trick
to finding the area quick.

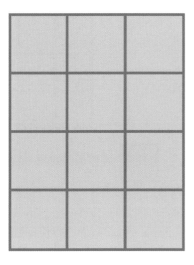

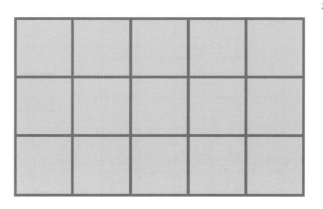

$3 \times 5 = 15$

Area = 15 square units

$4 \times 3 = 12$

Area = 12 square units

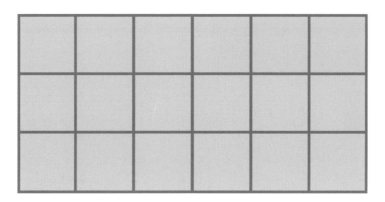

$3 \times 6 = 18$

Area = 18 square units

Find the area of each shape. Once the area is found, be sure to include the size of each unit square found inside.

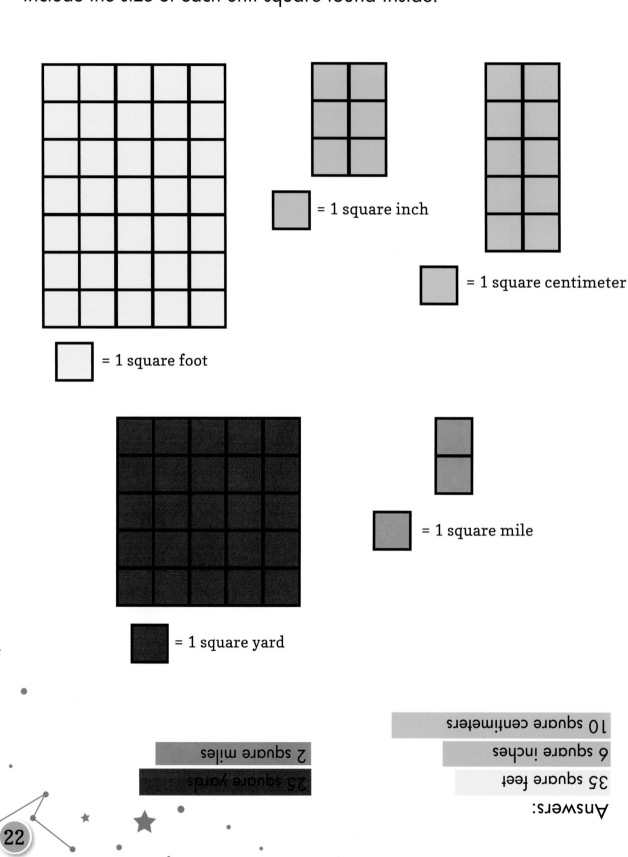

= 1 square inch

= 1 square centimeter

= 1 square foot

= 1 square mile

= 1 square yard

Answers:
35 square feet
6 square inches
10 square centimeters
25 square yards
2 square miles

22

Let's give area a try
without showing the square units inside.

To find the area, multiply the measure of the base by the measure of the height.

4 centimeters

8 centimeters

$$8 \times 4 = 32$$

Area = 32 square centimeters

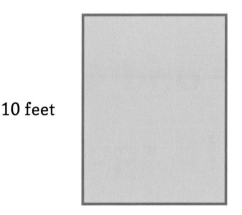

10 feet

5 feet

$$5 \times 10 = 50$$

Area = 50 square feet

Distributive Property

Thanks to the **distributive property**, you can split up a shape and simply add the areas you create.

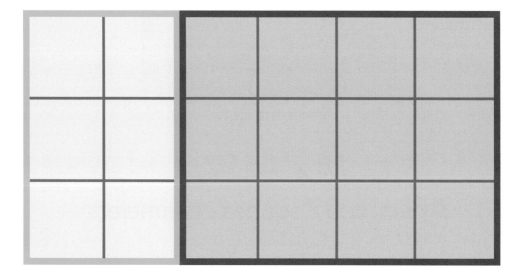

2 × 3 and 4 × 3

6 + 12 = 18 square units

Find the area of each rectangle using the
distributive property.

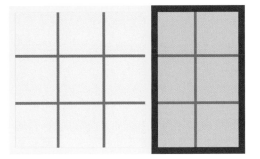

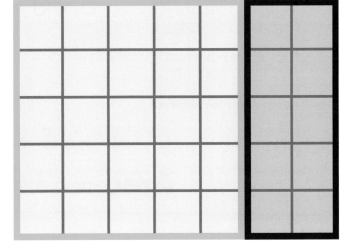

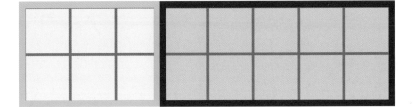

When a shape goes in too many directions for you to take.
Break it into shapes so you can find the area without mistake.

Add the areas together to equal the total area of the shape.

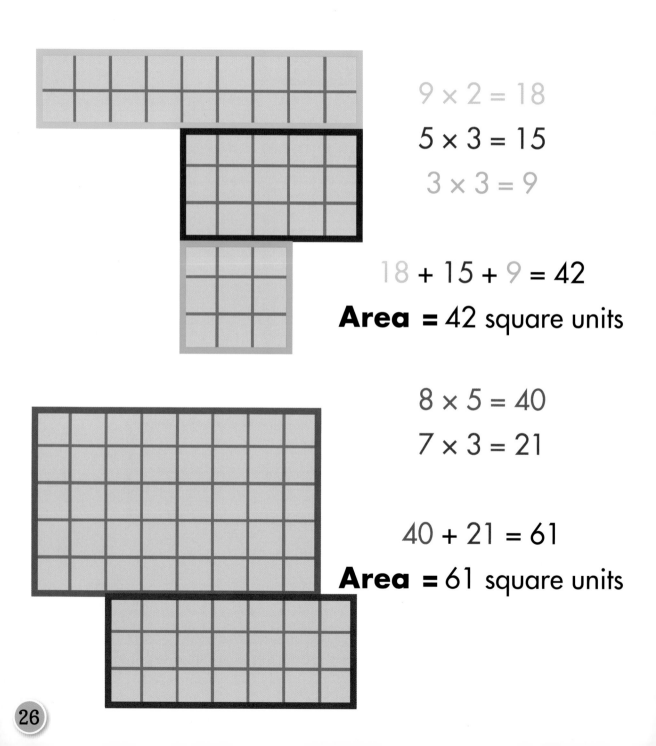

$9 \times 2 = 18$

$5 \times 3 = 15$

$3 \times 3 = 9$

$18 + 15 + 9 = 42$

Area $= 42$ square units

$8 \times 5 = 40$

$7 \times 3 = 21$

$40 + 21 = 61$

Area $= 61$ square units

Find the area of each shape.

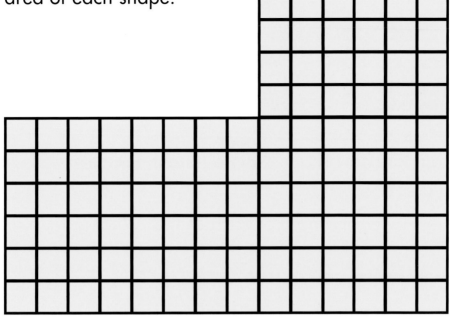

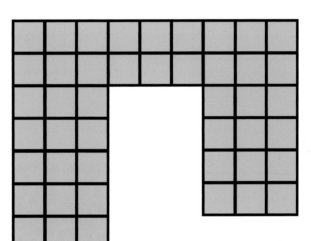

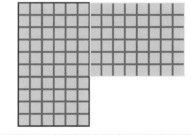

PERIMETER AND AREA PATTERNS

Time to compare how shapes with different perimeters can have matching areas.

Find the perimeter and area of each shape. What pattern do you see?

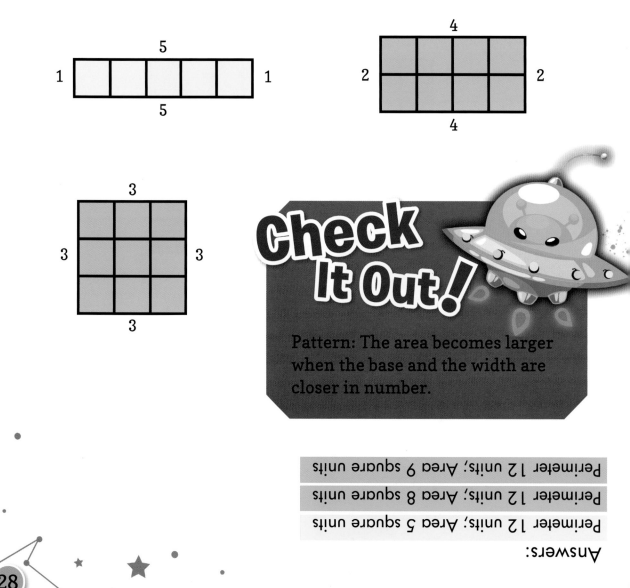

Pattern: The area becomes larger when the base and the width are closer in number.

Time to compare how shapes with matching perimeters can have different areas.

Find the perimeter and area of each shape. What pattern do you see?

Answers:

Perimeter 24 units; Area 20 square units
Perimeter 24 units; Area 27 square units
Perimeter 24 units; Area 32 square units
Perimeter 24 units; Area 36 square units

29

GLOSSARY

area (AIR-ee-uh): the number of square units covering a flat surface

dimensions (duh-MEN-shuhns): a measure in one direction

distributive property (dih-STRIB-yuh-tiv PROP-ur-tee): multiplying a group of numbers is equal to multiplying each number separately

height (hite): the measure from the base to the top of a shape

length (lengkth): how long something is

parallel (PA-ruh-lel): lines that remain the same distance apart and will never intersect

parallelograms (pa-ruh-LEL-uh-grams): a quadrilateral with opposite sides that are equal and parallel

perimeter (puh-RIM-uh-tur): the distance around a shape

points (POINTS): exact locations with no dimension

polygon (POL-ee-gon): a flat, closed shape with three or more straight sides

quadrilateral (kwahd-ruh-LAT-ur-uhl): a polygon with four sides

3-dimensional (THREE duh-MEN-shuhn-uhl): having three measures of length, width, and height

2-dimensional (TOO duh-MEN-shuhn-uhl): having two measures of length and width

width (WIDTH): the distance from one side of a shape to the other

INDEX

WEBSITES TO VISIT

www.crickweb.co.uk/ks2numeracy-shape-and-weight.html

www.sheppardsoftware.com/mathgames/geometry/shapeshoot/
   ClosedShapesShoot.htm

www.mrnussbaum.com/grade_3_standardsperimeter/

ABOUT THE AUTHOR

Lisa Arias is a math teacher who lives in Tampa, Florida with her husband and two children. Her out-of-the-box thinking and teaching style guided her toward becoming an author. She enjoys playing board games and spending time with family and friends.

Meet The Author!
www.meetREMauthors.com

PHOTO CREDITS: Cover: © sololos, jehsomwang; Page 4: © Snezhana Togoi

Edited by: Jill Sherman

Cover and Interior design by: Tara Raymo

Library of Congress PCN Data

Galactic Geometry: Two-Dimensional Figures / Lisa Arias
(Got Math!)
ISBN 978-1-62717-708-5 (hard cover)
ISBN 978-1-62717-830-3 (soft cover)
ISBN 978-1-62717-943-0 (e-Book)
Library of Congress Control Number: 2014935585

Printed in the United States of America, North Mankato, Minnesota

Also Available as: